D1564239

PROOF YOU'RE NOT ALONE

Anna Barba Stettler

PROLOGUE

Take a look, my darling
At all those who talk about
The things that no one talks about
They've come so far, you know
Why don't we run ahead, my darling?
We'll hold hands and talk about
The things that no one talks about
That no one talks about
And show them how far they've left to go

ALL THE LOST GENERATIONS

We're all comrades
Of one lost generation or another
Hemingway
Fitzgerald
Cummings
Slaphappy and hungry twenty-somethings
Of present day and days of yore
We *come of age* into the bygone notion
But untamed children still
Wandering the front lines
Of a revolution of questions
Constricted under an armor
Of irrelevant answers

ANXIETY

It's the itch
I can't scratch
But I do
I can't help it
I have to
Even now that I'm bleeding
And infected
And scarred
And bruised

ARSONISTS

Fuck it
Maybe we are arsonists like they say
We can spit out words like
Ecosystem
Soil
Health
Until we're blue in the face
But they can't hear us
They're too busy guarding fields
That aren't theirs to claim
So, fuck it
Our kids will need these fields
To grow their food
Let's burn them anyway

ART

Art doesn't paint the face of the canvas
Or rhyme the words of the poem
It doesn't caress the curves of the sculpture
Or dance through the frames of the film
It beats stronger than that
Art transcends its craft
It lumps in throats
And chills spiderwebs up spines
It races hearts
And pulls grenade pins in minds

ARTOLOGY

I'd fancy a visit with an artologist
How lovely would that be
A doctor of books and museums and music
Of movies and even cheeky TV
Someone to listen to the hard parts of my heart
And prescribe art to soften me
Stories that speak in ways conversations can't
But ways I so desperately need
Art is a drug powerful enough
To treat the symptoms of chronic humanity
And if only for a moment
Set a most tangled mind free
Imagine such a labor of love
To practice artology

BABY STEPS

It's like
I can't help but try
To wrap my mind
Around the big picture
But I get so overwhelmed by the scope
That I'm paralyzed
I can't make
Or see
Any progress
So I lose hope

BACKGROUND NOISE

In times like these
It's easy to ignore our instincts
We can forget we have them
Think we don't need them
Because we're so
Advanced
Civilized
Superior
Informed
But they're even more important now
Because the background noise is so loud
Louder than it ever has been before

BAD GUYS

You're the good guy
They're the bad guys
It's an enticing narrative
And it sells
But there and then
You're left
Still lost and a few dollars less
Asking yourself
If it ever really helped

BALANCE

Balance isn't an equation
That can simply be solved
Even by the most capable
Mathematicians in the world
You just have to feel it out
And adjust it constantly
Day in
And day out

THE BALLET

There's an uncomfortable truth
In the stories so beautifully told
By the ballet
Because outside the theater
On the streets
We're the dancers
But without the grace
Life forces us
Up onto our toes
And like the dancers in the show
Who've broken and bloodied their toes
While they trained
We feel all the pain

BATSHIT CRAZY

I empathize with everyone
But before you crown me a princess of peace
I mean
Everyone
Even the batshit crazies
Especially the batshit crazies

BEAR HUNT

The way past our feelings
Is through them

BELONGING

Control disguises itself
As the promise of belonging
But pay attention
And it'll give itself away
It'll ask you to forfeit
The things that
Already belong to you
In exchange

BIG, BIG WORLD

There's a big, big world out there
And it's going to be okay
Even when it's not
It is
Even when my world stops
The world out there
That's so much bigger than mine
Still spins

Anna Barba Stettler

BLACK HOLE

You can't see us
But we're right here with you
That black hole of the night
The one with the spiraling debris
That eats your mind
Swallowed us too
I know you already know
We may well be on our way
To nowhere and never
But what of that chance
That this monster will spit us out
Someday
Somewhere
Together

16

BONDED

We'll walk through heaven and hell
On earth together
We'll find ourselves over and over again
And sometimes we'll just get lost
But even that
Isn't all bad
Because it's the hardest things
That bond us
The strongest
As long as we stay soft

BROKEN

The world didn't break me
It lied to me
I broke myself because I believed it

BROKEN ROAD TO SUCCESS

It's harder now than ever
To follow the rules into success
And easier now than ever
To build it by breaking them
I suppose it always has been

BURN

A fire burned at the edge of town
And the townspeople worked tirelessly each day
Filling pails of water and pouring them over the fire
Keeping the destruction at bay

A young offender stood nearby
And snickered with his friends
He watched the townspeople tend to the fire
But roasted marshmallows instead

Change
The townspeople said to him
Be good

Years later he returned
Grown and set to protect his town's livelihood
He addressed the townspeople
Pail of water in hand
I've changed
He said
I'm good

You're too late
The townspeople spat
Struck his pail and watched it spill
Then turned to pour their own pails of water
Over the fire that burned ravenously still

BULLIES

They're the ones who laugh
At the things that aren't funny
And accuse those who don't
Of having no sense of humor
Of being freaks
They're the ones who make light of
The things that are heavy
And accuse those who struggle
Of being weak
But it's their souls
That cower and hide
In the corners of their minds
So afraid of their emotions
That they can't even think

BUS STOP

She waited
Arms folded
Legs crossed
Sitting on a wood slat bench
At an abandoned bus stop
She was pretty and pleasant enough
But her eyes were empty
And her mind was small
She was thirty- or forty- or fifty-something
And she had never been wrong

BUTTERFLIES

Butterflies endure
In cocoons as their wings grow
Ever intricate

CANCEL CULTURE

The good doesn't make the bad okay
But luckily for us
The bad doesn't take the good away

I think we're all a little afraid
Of the others deciding
We're bad one day
And hell
They'd probably be right in a lot of ways
But for everything else
They'd have just misunderstood

Still
Our work matters
Our art matters
And hard as they'd try
They couldn't write off our good

CATCH TWENTY-TWO

It's hard
To hear people talk about mental health
Now that they're doing well
But it makes sense
It's a lot easier to talk
About how we were lost
Once we're out of the woods
Hoping someone will share
When they're in the thick of despair
Is a something of a catch twenty-two

Why would we believe our words are worthy
When we feel like we're nothing
Like we're worthless?
When we're so insecure
We want to disappear
How are we supposed to have courage?

It would be hard enough
To stand in front of
A crowd of judgmental eyes
And take off our clothes
So how is it anything but an impossible ask
To expose
Our more vulnerable parts
Our deeper-than-skin parts?

Maybe the people who are talking now
Really do know
Or maybe they don't
But they're taking about it
People are talking about it
We're talking about it
And that means
There's hope

THE CAVEAT

Let's call good
God
And evil
The devil
For relatability's sake
They're always sending us signs
Out of nowhere
From everywhere
It's how they communicate
But there's a caveat
It's so easy to misinterpret the signs
It's been that way since the beginning of time
Who sent what
What they mean
It's up to us to decide
Sometimes we think we know
But we don't
We're only human after all
And we're full of pride

CHEERS

Perhaps it's already been said
In some other way on some other day
So what?
Say it again
Perhaps a cocktail of truth
Mixed with the nuances of your recipe
Will finally quench the insatiable thirst
Of a parched soul wandering desperately

COLORBLIND

I was young and naive
And the world was black and white
Most everything was wrong
But it was okay
Because I was right
I trusted that as I grew older
Time would paint my life in color
But my vision is beginning to fade
I don't know much of anything now
And all I see is gray

CONSUMERISM

We all want things
We're human
Of course we do
But do you consume the things
You have
And want
And need
Or do they consume you?

CRAVINGS AND HUNGER

What I'm hungry for
And what I crave
Are not the same
But how do I shush
The off-key karaoke voices of the cravings
Enough to hear
The soft melody of the hunger pangs?

CROSSROADS

The greatest minds of their times
Weren't always great
Back before they were world-renowned
They probably started at a crossroads
Between an epiphany and a nervous breakdown

DARK CLOUDS AND ALL THAT SHIT

They want to be brave
But all the things they've been feeling
Seem impossible to articulate
So they speak in dried-up, old clichés

I get it
And I believe them anyway

DEATH DOESN'T HAVE TO BE SCARY

We're human
A relationship with mortality is a given
Some endure it
And keep it at a distance
Others enjoy it
And make it hot and intimate
The closer you are
The more it sparks
If you let it inside of you
You'll set off fireworks
You'll love harder
Smile wider
Breathe deeper
Sleep sounder
See clearer
Live freer
There's no sense in fearing the inevitable
We're going to die
We might as well go out with a bang
And light up the whole damn sky

DEFENSE IS THE MOST REASONABLE RESPONSE TO AN ATTACK

You can't close your mind
And use it to bash another's open
They'll just reinforce it
And it will hurt
Them
You
The situation
You'll only make it worse

DON'T LISTEN WHEN THEY SAY YOU DON'T HAVE THE VOCABULARY TO PARTICIPATE

There were a million scholars
We don't remember
And they had vocabularies
That would blow you away
Their credentials died with them
But they were never as relevant
As anyone thought they were anyway
The people we do remember
We remember
Because they had something to say

Anna Barba Stettler

DREAMS AND TIME

Sometimes
Oftentimes
Your dreams come true
For someone else
So much faster and easier
Than they have yet to for you
But there's a bit of truth
Don't you think
In that tired, old cliché
The one about the things worth having
And how easily they came

DUDE

It comes so effortlessly
To accept my dream worlds
As reality
No matter how nonsensical and skewed
But when I wake
Into a world of science and practicality
It's consciousness that's confusing
I'm tellin' ya
Life's a trip
Dude

EARTHSONG

The whistle of her winds
The rustle of her palms
Her song is her dance
And her dance is her song
And the moon
Shines a bright spotlight overhead
And the stars
Give their twinkling applause

EASY THINGS

You can do hard things
But if you're anything like me
Here's your reminder that
You can do easy things too
If those simple, menial tasks
Make your palms sweat
If you're paralyzed and stressed
Over *nothing*
I'm right there with you

EMOTIONS

In theory
The ocean is a terrifying mystery
The one thing I know
Is that it could swallow me whole
A logical person might avoid it
But they'd never find out what happens
When you swim out a little way
When you embrace it
It embraces you right back
And your fear dissipates with the waves
It's exhilarating and comforting all the same
I hope I always have the courage
To immerse myself
And feel what it's like
To be one with the ocean
And hope I can always make out
The horizon in the distance
Where the ocean parallels my emotions

EVEN WHEN YOU CAN'T SEE IT

Even when it fogs over
Even when you can't see it at all
Even when you lose hope
And feel alone
And impossibly small
I hope you know
You have purpose

EVERYTHING ELSE

If we could cure
What ails our mental health
Might that solve
Most everything else?

EVIL IS LIKE GRAVITY

Evil drags us down
We know that
But I think it's often misunderstood
Sure
It would kill us
Without the opposing force of its counterpart
But then again
So would good
Good alone is weightless
We'd just float through space
It wouldn't be much of a human life
And eventually
We'd suffocate
Evil is like gravity
It's heavy
We feel it weighing on our tired bodies
On our souls
But together with good it grounds us
Allows us to live in the world
To be human
To be whole

FEMINIST

He told me he was bored with me
Disenchanted with lukewarm complacency
Offended me until I knew
That my dreams matter too

FLYING BLIND

I'm human, alive
And it's totally dark inside
I'm flying blind
And the only way to survive my mind
Is to look behind my eyes
And learn to see without sight

FOR BETTER

We'll confront each other in front of our kids
That's a promise we snuck into our vows
We'll teach our sons to oppose benevolently
And our daughters to stand their ground
We'll show them a candid and courageous love
Topsy-turvy
Harum-scarum
Helter-skelter
We'll fight and make up and kiss in the rain
For better or for worse
Forever

FOR THE ADVENTURE

He was a photographer
Studied and learned
He went all in
Climbed mountains and scaled cliffs
Anything for the shot
And some of his work was really good
But mostly
It was just pretty okay
And he was drained
So he threw in the towel
Gave it all up
And chased adventure instead
He took a few photos along the way

And they were great

FREE WILL

Forces of good and evil
Exist within me
Within my soul
Evil forces me to stop
And consciously breathe
And remind myself
I'm the one in control

GHOST STORIES

What stays with you
When the ghost stories have been told
After the storylines are closed?
The stories?
Or the ghosts?

GOD

Perhaps it's your god
Who commands the universe
Or perhaps it's mine
Perhaps the distance between them
Spans a waste of limited time

GOLD

Gold isn't gold
It's hard and it's cold
Take my hand if you want
It's empty but
It's soft and warm and yours to hold

THE GOOD GROUNDED

Adventure is out there
I said
And he said
When it's feasible and fair
I'll go with you
And then he took my hand and took me home
And showed me
It's right here too

THE GOOD KIND OF LOST

It won't always be like this
Someday
You'll find your way back
Not home
Or wherever the final destination is
That you're supposed to go
But back to your path
And you'll still be lost
But in a good way
And you'll be glad
You're not dead
And you'll *want*
To stick around
And see how it ends

GRAPES AND PEOPLE

Grapes are fuel
When you eat them off the vine
They'll nourish your soul
When you turn them into wine
But if a dog eats them
It may not survive
People are toxic
To certain people
They aren't toxic people

GRAVITY

I was born into death's atmosphere
Life's ironic in that way
It's so clear and beautiful above the clouds
But I'm falling faster every day

THE GRIND

We'll probably have to work jobs
We don't particularly like
It's life
It's the grind
It's fine
That's why cubicles and offices
Are lined with family photos and framed mantras
And if you climb high enough
Even windows looking outside
It's a tradition
We forget to question
But the answer is simple
We have to remind ourselves
Why

GROWING OLD TOGETHER

I dream of growing old as fuck with you
Of how sexy you'll look
With your pants hiked up too high
Of dying my hair
That iconic shade of grandma blue
Of our leather faces
That the sun has spotted
That worries have wrinkled
That laughs have lined
Etched with the adventure map
Of a discretely epic life

GROWING UP

I was a child and they were adults
It was so easy to tell
So obvious before
Maybe that's how I know I've grown up
I can't spot the difference anymore

GUILT

Of all the bags
I push and drag
The heaviest is guilt

THE HAND I WAS DEALT

I can't change the hand I've been dealt
I've tried
And I've bitched and I've whined
And all that's been good for
Is wasting my time
I can play my hand though
Strategically
Creatively
Authentically
I can own it
Because it's mine
And in doing so
I can change the outcome
Of the game

HASTY CONCLUSIONS

I jumped off a boat
And swam out to a rock
But now the boat is gone
And I know
That in one way or another
The tide will come

HAVOC

They're brave
Those who share their stories
Who were, are even
Blinded by worthlessness
Hopelessness
Depression
But amidst that darkness
I still see
I'm afraid
Because I'm dangerous
I start to think
Maybe I'm the one
Who should end it
Spare everyone the havoc I could wreak
With just one motion
If I lost control
For just one second

HE STAYED QUIET

He was loved
As much as anyone's kid ever was
But he watched his people
Watch other people
And judge
So he didn't tell them
He couldn't tell them
How was he to know
He was different?
How was he to know
They would've helped him?

HEADSPACE

Tiny, trivial things
Tend to occupy so much of my mind
And I'm at a perpetual loss
Unless I constantly remind myself
That my headspace is as big as the sky

HEROES

A girl who'd never been misunderstood
Couldn't empathize with anomalies like that
A boy who'd never run scared
Couldn't reason with ghosts like that
A woman who'd never ventured alone
Couldn't show the lost they belong like that
A man who'd never gone hungry or cold
Couldn't make a house a home like that
A mother who hadn't grown up too soon
Couldn't guard her baby's childhood like that
A father who'd never been broken or bruised
Couldn't kiss the boo-boos better like that
And a hero who'd never been hurt
Couldn't change the world for the better like that

HIDDEN FACES

I've seen the hidden faces
Since I was a child
You know
Like the ones etched into the patterns
On bathroom tiles
And all the while
They were passive and kind
But not anymore
Now all the faces scream
And I don't know if they're evil or
Just scared like me
Or maybe
Scared for me
Or maybe
Scared of me

HINDSIGHT

Hindsight isn't twenty-twenty
It's hazardous as hell
Through the rearview mirror
Everything's inverted
And smaller than it felt

HOLLYWOOD ENDING

Cocoons smoke and burn
The same as leaves
When you take a magnifying glass
And hold it over them in the sun
It can happen to people too
When their spotlight is magnified too much
Before they've even had a chance
To become who they're supposed to become

HOSTAGE

I'm being held hostage
I feel trapped
But the scariest part
Is that I'm my captor
The only one
Who can set me free
Is me
And I don't know how to do that

Anna Barba Stettler

HOT AND COLD

I need to remember
When I'm in the darkest places
Just how quickly
Everything in my mind
My whole outlook on life
Changes

HOW TO KNOW WHEN TO LISTEN

What do you do
When you feel like your voice isn't being heard?
Do you amplify it
Or do you get discouraged
Or
Do you just shut up
And listen
And learn?

HOW TO SPEND OUR TIME

We're always
Living
And always
Dying
But not always
In the same proportions

HUMANITIES

We pit good and evil
God and the devil
Against one another as enemies
As if they'd play our mortal game
Perhaps they're friends
Perhaps they're lovers
Perhaps they're one and the same

I HOPE YOU DIE

I hope you die
Of old age that is
When it's your time
Without imminent
Impending
Inevitable
Death
Would there really be life?

IDENTITY

If your city isn't serving you
You move somewhere else
You paint and redecorate your house
To make it your own
But what are you supposed to do
When the body that was given to you
Doesn't feel like home?

IF IT'S CONTROVERSIAL

Even if
Especially if
They don't like it
And they think it's bizarre
If it's controversial
All the better
All the best things are

IMAGINE

I want to see the world
Like my children do
With an innate appreciation
They don't just see it with their eyes
They see it with their imagination
And that's how we can change it

IMPACT

If you help one person
It'll be worth it
But that's only true
If you don't hurt another doing it

IN TUNE

Emotional people
Are called out for being emotional
Like it's a character flaw
It's not
Being in tune with your emotions
Is like the way a piano needs to be tuned
To hear the beauty of its songs
If it's been neglected
The sound is off
Those who aren't in tune with their emotions
Know it
Though they'd probably describe it as
Being strong
Or *having balls*
They convince themselves
They don't need music
So they choose not to play anything at all

INSTINCTS

It's almost natural
To lose yourself
In fear of what the world thinks
But trust yourself
The universe speaks to you
Through your instincts

IT IS

Sometimes
We set out to do good
With all the passion in the world
But somewhere along the way
Our once pure motivation
Becomes a little tainted
And we're forced to grow up
When we realize passion isn't enough
To carry us all the way
And we doubt whether
Our intent was ever
Good in the first place
So we get discouraged
Left to wonder if it's even worth it

IT MATTERS

If you think broadly enough
Some philosophers say
We're meaningless
None of it matters at all
But I think that's a phenomenon
That happens when
People try to think so impossibly big
That their minds implode
And become small

IT WAS TOO MUCH TO BE THEM TOO

The slow return to consciousness
Is the dreamiest part of my dreams
When all the roles I was playing
All the people I was projecting
Collapse back into my body
And I realize
I'm just me
The relief
Is so profound
It soothes me right back to sleep

Anna Barba Stettler

IT WASN'T A WASTE

I had to be
The one to dream the dream
To fight hard for it
To discover for myself
That it wasn't for me

IT'S NOT ALWAYS A CRY FOR HELP

I promise you have time
To listen
Before you force
A wise reply
Or try to muster up
Some wasn't-asked-for advice
When we open up about our mental health
If you're listening at all
It isn't so hard to tell
If it really is a cry for help
Or if we're just trying to help someone else

IT'S NOT JUST YOU

Awkward people don't exist
Only awkward interactions
Between people who haven't clicked

IT'S NOT WHY
BUT IT IS

My shortcomings
And controversial decisions
Aren't why I feel guilty
I'm surprisingly okay with them
And that's why I feel guilty
I don't know how to be okay
With being okay
With them

IT'S OKAY FOR A WHILE

Even when we're grown
Sometimes all we can do to cope
Is close our eyes
And that's okay
For a while
We have to face the world eventually though
Like a person trapped in a pitch-black cave
We'll go blind if we don't

IT'S REAL

Real
Is subjective
Sometimes a desire or a fear or a dream
Feels more real than anything you've ever lived
More real than anything you've ever seen

JUST A STUMBLE

How many times have you stumbled
Without falling?
How many times have you fallen
Without breaking?
How many times have you broken
Without dying?
Only you know how hard
The things you're going through are
But you're not dead yet
Keep going
Keep trying

KIDS TODAY

But the kids

Their world
Was never supposed to be this big

Their awkwardness was obvious enough
Back when they genuinely believed
That they went to high school
With the queen bee

But now
They know
They don't

Now
They're exposed
To everything

KNOTS

It's like
My head can't handle
The weight of my thoughts
So they fall
Down to my back and
Tie themselves into knots
They get bigger
Pull tighter
And it hurts
So bad
But I'll be damned
If I let anyone hear me complain
So I keep quiet
Break down in private
So I can be anything
But the pathetic drama queen
With the phantom pain

LABEL THEM LAZY

They were paralyzed
In ways too clever to be seen
Undetectable by the swankiest X-ray machines
If we'd listened with all we had
We could've heard the words they couldn't say
But we had our own mountains to climb
And problems to solve
So we labeled them lazy
It was the easiest way to write them off

LEGACY

It's ironic and crazy
But maybe
When the future looks back on my life
Right now will be the time
That inspires the most
Because I was nobody's *goals*
I was stressed and
Less than
Stable
And that's relatable
And they'll say
She made a million mistakes
But she turned out okay
She was just like us
And she was enough
And we are enough

LISTENING

I'm listening
Just not in the way I'm supposed to
But the visionaries might like that
Maybe they'll say
That's just what I hoped she'd do

THE LITTLE THINGS

We have a habit
Of saying
All that really matters is...
But it's okay when
That isn't true
It's okay when
The most important thing
Isn't the only thing that matters
It's okay when
The little things matter too

LOVE

You can give them the pieces of your heart
Without breaking it
Or trading your soul
And you can give them the world
Without taking it
As your own

LOVEBIRDS

How easily
He swept me off my feet
Once I unloaded
The weight I put on his shoulders
Trying to make him my everything

MAGIC AND LOGIC

Our world
Outer space
It's all a nonsensical place
We can make sense of it
Where there is sense to be made
And everything else
Is perfectly illogical to explain
And it's best that way

MAKING SPACE

Falling out of love
Was a shit pie to the face
But it wasn't the end
It was life making space
To fall in love all over again

MATERIAL DREAMS

My material dreams finally came true
And I panicked
Because there was no cloud nine
The world told me to dream those dreams
But they were never really mine
And everyone thought
Wow
Look at her
Look what she has
She's so lucky
She'll be fine

MATTER

How might I matter
She asked the sky
In a world that might not?
Her gaze held steady and distant
But the tears flowed
Behind her eyes and into her throat
My child
Whispered the wind
Just like the sun and the earth
And all else that will die
You matter because you're alive

THE MEMORIES FADE
THE FEELINGS STAY

I saw a sleep psychologist
In a dream

To have dreams about
How fucked up your dreams are
How fucked up must someone be?

My memory of the dream is fuzzy of course
But I perfectly articulated my problem to her
It was something about how I felt when I woke

About how I longed to wake
Feeling rested and refreshed
Instead of just itchy and gross

THE MENTAL ILLNESS CLUB

It's not some fucked-up fraternity
There are no bids or cuts
It's not something you have to pledge
How many members
Do we have to induct into
The Mental Illness Club
After they're already dead?

MIRROR

We all carry a mirror
That no one else can see
But we can't see ourselves clearly
If our mirror is cracked
Mine is cracked
And I feel it breaking into shards of glass
I'm trying to hold it together
But it's cutting into my hands
In theory I know
I should drop it
Just let it go
Get a new one
Relax
And I don't know why
I try and I try
But I just
Can't

MIRROR OF STRIDER

Not all those who don't wander aren't lost

MISUNDERSTOOD

I'd never felt more misunderstood
Than when they misunderstood
My understanding
For misunderstanding

MOMENT

A moment
That's all it is
Half a second, maybe
Or even half a century
When you're in it
It's infinite
But once it's over
That's all it ever was
A moment

MOMENT IN THE SUN

Young dreamers
Chase their moment in the sun
For seasons of their lives
And we let them
Because who would we be
To stand in their way
And some of them
The ones who run fast enough
Push hard enough
Actually catch the light
And they feel the warmth
For a moment
Maybe even for a day
But the sun sets
As it always does
And when it does
Their moment stops mattering as much
We should tell them
Because sometimes
They're too lost in the dark to see
That their fight
Still matters to the people they inspired
That's their legacy

MONSTERS

Monsters will tell you
Monsters aren't real
They'll comfort you
Convince you there's no need to run
They know if you did
You'd outpace them 10-to-1

MOTHER EARTH

My body belongs to her
She molded a piece of herself
Into a temporary temple
For my soul to dwell
Through her sufferance I materialized
Able to walk and see and work
Given a chance to make a difference
And love the other parts of her
In time my body will return to her
I must surrender this life forever
And if my soul is still whole and I'm able to hope
I'll hope I changed her for the better

MY BABY

Holding you in my arms
Is like holding onto time
You're your very own
And you're also mine

MY FOREVER

All of my yesterdays
Todays
Tomorrows
And somedays
Start and end with you
You're my stroke of midnight
My be-everywhere-at-once
Wish come true

NATURE AND NURTURE

I think it's a bit ironic
The nature of
The nature versus nurture debate
Like it's black and white
Either/or
When it comes to how we come into
Our behaviors and traits
But I think it's always
The combining of the two
That results in everything we know
In everything we are
And in everything we do

NEVER REALLY READY

When it comes to the important things
That push me to act out of my comfort zone
I've always said
I'll be ready when...
But the time passes
As it always does
And *when* always comes
And I'm never ready by then

NEVER TOO FAR GONE

The further you're gone
The more you've left to find
There's no *too far gone*

NICE GUYS

I played by the rules
Followed the proper steps
In the proper order
And found all the clues
Just like I was supposed to do

And I finally found the hidden key
I can see it
But it's locked inside
So I need to axe down the door
Like the rebels did from the beginning
And now I'm just behind

NIGHTMARE

Waking up old and tired
Having slept on all my dreams
Would be a nightmare

NOT TELLING YOUR WHOLE TRUTH
IS NOT A LIE

There will always be details they won't know
Neither you nor they have that kind of time
So share the details you want
Or don't
You don't owe it to them
Protecting your privacy is not a lie

NOT TOO LATE

They might be right
It might take a lifetime of study and practice
To become great
But hardly anyone is great
To be any good
Takes hardly any time at all
It's not too late
You're not too late

NOT YET

Not now
Doesn't mean
Not ever
It may still happen
And the timing may be even better
Take the space
Give yourself the grace
To grieve
Once the chapter is closed for good
But it's not over yet
Now is not the time for that

NUGGETS

Nuggets
Of wisdom and happiness and peace
Are hidden in plain sight
They're all around us
Regardless of who you are
Or what path you walk in life

ON COMPETITION

I wish they'd told me
When I set out to win
That I'd already lost
But they cheered me on
They didn't know better
All they knew
Was that they'd lost too

ON QUESTIONS AND FAITH

If the truly faithful knew your doubt
They'd tell you it's okay
That they welcome your questions
That you don't have to be afraid
You'll hurt them by rocking their faith
How else can they test its strength?
If it falls
It wasn't very strong in the first place
And something else
Something less gentle
Would have knocked it over anyway

THE ONES WHO JUMP

We didn't see it coming
And we're dumbfounded when we're too late
As if they passed us running
Toward what didn't have to be their fate
But we all walk a path in life
And their path was a bridge
And for who knows how long
They lingered along the edge
They never held a sign
That read
Hey guys
I don't know if I'm gonna make it
No
They were preoccupied
Taking it
As long as they could take it
True
We didn't know where their path had led
But what's maybe even more
They didn't know about ours
Or that we'd walked that very bridge before

OVERANALYSIS

A million mistakes
Leave me dazed but awake
Stumbling over my mind
One foot in front of the other
Isn't so simple
When you're trying to move forward
And backtrack at the same time

PAIN

They chose to leave
But that doesn't mean
They wanted to die
I think they were searching for
Something
Anything
Even nothing
Less painful than life

PAIN IS PAIN

Loss is loss
Yes
It is
But also
No
It's not
It doesn't all weigh the same
But there's no arbitrary level of loss
You need to prove
To validate your pain

PARIS

Paris is magic
Because it isn't
It changed my life
Because it didn't
I fell deeply for the city of love
In time
As is true of true love
I couldn't fall to its depths
At first sight

PARISIAN LOVE LETTER

My favorite view of Paris
Is a perspective that can only be seen
From the champagne deck of a river cruise
Traveling up and down the Seine

Paris is exquisite from every which angle
Spanning her left bank and her right
But afloat along the river that divides them
She'll let you see inside her mind

You'll have only a moment to look too closely
At the complexity of the bridges that connect her city
Squirm slightly overwhelmed before the boat journeys forward
Throughout time those connections have crumbled
Under the heavy baggage of her history
But true to her promise they're always restored

You'll see flickers of tiny people crossing her bridges
Bouncing from park to building
And pedaling her synapses of streets
They're part of her
They're the signals and brain waves
That communicate to make her think

To fall for Paris is to fall for people
Past our deadly pitfalls all the way to our potential
For our hearts and desires and the things we're capable of
The wonderful, horrible, mundane, extraordinary things
All of them
Worthy of love

PAST, PRESENT AND/OR FUTURE

She dwells in the past
And daydreams of the future
And she doesn't even realize how long it's been
Since she's been outside
To feel the sensations of the present
Like the warmth of the sun on her sequestered skin

PILLARS

I stand amongst ancient ruins
Marveling at the remnants of an age-old time
The mortals and their monuments perished
But the pillars
What they stood for
Survived

POLITICS

Are we fighting
Over the roots of the cause
Or over weeds that were planted
As a clever distraction
From what's really going on?

POTTERS AND PILLAGERS

The pillagers beat me down to break me
To cherry-pick the valuable parts and take me
The potters beat me down to make me
To strengthen my foundation and wake me
But they all wore masks
And the beat-down felt all the same upon my back
So I learned to brace in place
Too scared to face the attack
Then, ever sore and further hunched
I begrudgingly forged my path
I happened upon
The odd pillager and potter along the way
They pulled down their masks
And revealed whether they'd taken me for ceramic
Or believed me to be clay
And so I came to know
A few who'd awaited my failure
And a few who'd believed I'd succeed
They granted me a closure
I didn't know I didn't need
And when I got where I was going
I finally understood
That it never mattered
Who was right and who was wrong
The only truth that ever mattered
Was what I was made of all along

PRACTICAL FAILURE

I know what it's like
To perpetually fail
At all the practical things you try
All the while knowing in your heart
That one impractical thing
Is so right
That nothing else is

Chin up, darling
That's the curse of purpose
And the long road to get there
On the seemingly impossible terrain
Makes it all the more worth it

PURPOSE

Leave this place better than you found it
My mother told me when I was five
And too busy chasing lightning bugs
To complicate the *what for?*s and *why?*s

PUTTING OUT FIRES

Her child said
I want to be a firefighter someday
And she smiled
Because she knew
That no matter what
He would be
It's what we do
We're all firefighters in a way
We put out fires
Sometimes little fires
Sometimes big fires
Every day

QUALIFIED

Sometimes it's masked strangers
Hiding in the shadows
Sometimes it's someone you know
Even respect
Sometimes it's subtle
Sometimes it's backhanded
Sometimes it's direct
They'll question you
I'm not sure anyone knows just why
But they'll do their best
To make you question yourself
What makes you think you're qualified?
It may not be malicious
But they'll throw a roadblock or two in your way
Go ahead and use them
As stepping stones
And change the world anyway

QUARTER-LIFE CRISIS

The rational part
Of our brains
Fully develops
Around 25 or 26
Right around the time
We realize
We don't know shit

RAISING THE FUTURE

I want to raise up my children so well
That when you ask them
Who they want to be like when they grow up
They tell you
Themselves

REASONS

She said
I believe what I believe
For very specific reasons
And I'm not sure whether she knew
That everyone else does too

Anna Barba Stettler

RECIPE FOR FAILURE

Traditional suit
Traditional dress
Traditional vows to recite
It's all a bit of a disservice, really
Encouraging the young couple
To sketch out their marriage
In black and white

RELIEF

I don't ask the gods
For euphoria
I plead with them
For relief
I'm so tired
Of being so tired
Please
Just let me sleep

RIGHTEOUSNESS

Honor is found in doing right
But in being right
There's only pride

ROOTS

Even roots aren't permanent
You can dig them up
Just be careful
Not to dig a grave
Without proper
Care
Nourishment
Environment
You could kill the very thing
You're trying to save

ROSES ARE RED

Spring is fertile
Summer is bright
Fall is cozy
And winter is white
Sometimes it's too cold
Sometimes it's too warm
But the seasons will pass
And so will this storm

STAY-AT-HOME PARENT

What did I do all day?
It's our little secret
You're the only one who knows
And your developing mind will soon forget
But your soul won't

THE SCARIEST GHOSTS

Some people don't believe in ghosts
They denounce and deny them
To protect us
Or themselves
Or both
Their ghosts
Scare me the most

SCIENCE AND MAGIC

There are theories
Science
Devised to explain causation
Mechanisms to cope
With an innate discomfort
With uncertainty
Science bridges the gap
Between natural and supernatural
Magic
For what is magic
But phenomena not yet rationalized
And what is science
But rationalization of magic

THE SECRET TO LIFE

The secret to life
Will always be
The secret to life
Even if you know it
You can't share it
No matter how hard you try
We have to uncover it for ourselves
And if it's something we never find
I wonder if we finally do
Right before we die

SELFISH

What a paradox
A lovely Pandora's Box
To call the suicidal selfish
When in the end
A morsel of selfishness
Might have been
The antidote
That could've saved them

SHE WOULDN'T DREAM OF UNLEASHING IT

She was so afraid
Of becoming the monster in her head
That she killed it
The only way she knew how
If only she'd known
It wouldn't have
Couldn't have
Hurt anyone else
That it would have died
Had she just let it out

SIGNS

By the time I decided
To start listening to the universe
I already knew what it was going to say
It's been the background soundtrack to my life
That I've tried to tune out
But it plays on repeat every day

SLAVE TO TOMORROW

I fucked it up
Today is shot
There's always tomorrow
That's when
I'll try again
I'll start then
I'm human though
Humans fuck up every day
And I need to stop telling myself that shit
It's a harmless enough sentiment
Until I realize how long it's been
I'm a slave to tomorrow
And I'm decades in

SMALL WORRIES

Big people
Belittle the kids
And assume
They're carefree
Or at least they should be
But they're not
They chuckle at how small
Their own worries used to be
But they remember wrong
A small worry to a small person in a small world
Is just as heavy
As a big worry to a big person in a big world

SOMEDAY

Someday
When I have it all together
Or mostly together
Or somewhat together
Things will be different
And I'll write about this day
About this season
When I didn't

STAY

Sometimes
It's best
To granularly explain
Sometimes
It's best
To leave it unframed

Stay

STENCH

Of course we're our own worst critics
Who else has fought our battle
Long enough to admit
Just how bad the stench is
When we're knee-deep in the trenches
Of our own shit?

THE STING

Most things
Aren't part of a divine plan
They happen by chance
And people will judge you
For controlling what you can
But once you've felt the judgment
You realize
The sting really isn't so bad

Anna Barba Stettler

THE STRENGTH TO BREAK

We're broken
Alone
In the dark
And when we think it out loud
We can relax
And let ourselves fall apart
We can finally escape the mold
Of what we are
The more broken fragments
The better
All the more light we'll catch
When we piece ourselves together

STRONG

Maybe they live in your house
Maybe they live in your head
But your demons are real
And maybe no one else knows
Just how hard they hit
But you're still here
And there's beauty in that
And so much power
Being the only one who knows
Doesn't leave you all alone
When we look at each other
We'll know
That we're all
The only ones who know
How strong we really are

Anna Barba Stettler

STRONG AS SOFT

He learned
Through trial and error
That more often than not
They'd talk about the hard things after all
As long as he stayed soft

SUPER-SPREADER

Hard as the artist tried
To paint the difference between
The person who climbed to the height of the pandemic
And spat in faces
And the person who shamed others
For their feelings
The canvas stayed blank

TABOO

One day
The word *taboo*
Will describe the silly game of tag
Our ancestors used to play
With the truth

TEASE

You're not alone
Is just something people say
Clouds hang over them, too
They'll tell you
And detail the shades of gray
They mean well
But all too often
They'll tease vulnerability
And then play it safe
All the while I'm imploding
Dying for
A million times more
And it only drives home
That I am alone
More so, even
Than I felt before

TEETH

Guilt
True guilt
In its purest form
Rips its infinite sharp teeth through me
Like a hungry shark's brutal attack
But like a shark wouldn't eat me
It doesn't eat me
No
I'm no good
So there I am
There I'm left
In the middle of the ocean
Mangled and bleeding and broken
Drowning
Waiting for the other sharks
To attack

THAT'S NOT LOVE

I'd never felt it
I didn't know
I thought I could love the hardest
By breaking myself apart just so
To fill his voids
Like missing puzzle pieces
And it wouldn't matter
If I was broken
Because he would be whole

THAT'S NOT LOYALTY

You don't owe it
To the people you love
To help them
Carry their grudge

THEIR STORY AND YOURS

You can't write their story
It'll never work
It's self-serving
And they'll see through you
You'll paint yourself a jerk
They'll write you out of it
To spite you
And rightfully so
When they might have listened
To your story in the first place
The one about you
That you wrote

THEY PAVED THE WAY
BUT

They may
Have paved the way
But pavement doesn't last forever
It cracks
And erodes
It sinks into potholes
We have to maintain it
And even so
Eventually
We have to repave the road

THEY'LL LOSE THEMSELVES

It's scary to think about
How scared my children will be
When they come to that point in their lives
When they realize
They're utterly lost
But if that never happens for them
They'll never find themselves at all
And that's an even scarier thought

THICK SKIN

When it happened to them
I stood by their side
So when it happened to me
I thought they'd be just as horrified

But they weren't
They listed the reasons
Why their trial was harder instead
And what it all really boiled down to was
It was harder because it happened to them

But they never meant
To belittle and betray me like they did
They genuinely believed
Their hurt was worse
And I think that's because they could feel it

It's true
They shouldn't have accepted a loyalty
They couldn't return
But they're not bad
And they never were
They're just imperfect people
And that's not how most minds work
Especially when they're hurt
And anyway
It was me
I was the one who had everything to learn

THE THINGS WE WANT

We're wired to want things
We're humans
It's who we are
But when we start wanting
The things that aren't things
Like love and solutions and progress and peace
That when the sparks start
The good sparks

THOSE MOMENTS

I wish you a moment
That prompts you to address the sky
And declare you'd trade
A hundred years
Of blood, sweat and tears
For that lonely flicker in time
And that the sky
Might hear your heart
And rain those moments
All over your life

TIGHTROPE IN THE SKY

What about the people
Millions, maybe billions of people
Who are running for their lives
With so many immediate and tangible threats
They don't even know
They're running along a tightrope in the sky
I'm more fortunate
I have the luxuries of caution and time
What about the people
Who don't get to know
That if they were to fall
They'd die

TO CLEAR MY HEAD

I've been trying
To clear my head
Just like they said
But I've been going about it all wrong
They didn't mean empty it
When they said it
They meant defrost
And defog

TO LOVE A LIGHT

You're a light
Your goodness shines
For 10,000 miles
Maybe more
Words fail to describe
What it's like
To be close enough
To feel your warmth

TOO TIRED TO GO TO BED

It's that paralyzing time of night again
When I'm too tired to go to bed
So I sit
And stare
And scroll
And let the clock tick on instead

TREASURE

We'll find the treasure here somewhere
Or so we're told
We just have to sift through these mountains
Of jewels and pearls and gold

TREASURE HUNTERS

He knew he was supposed to
Hunt for treasure
But nobody told him
Treasures aren't things
He only learned
When joy sparkled in her moonlit eyes
And he saw
The most beautiful gems he'd ever seen

TRUE COLORS

When they've been hurt
They'll tell you
When people show you their true colors
Believe them
And that's true
For a while
But pay mind
To where they are in their lives
Leaves change colors
With the seasons

TRUTH AND LIES

Maybe God
Or good
Or whatever you want to call it
Is truth
And truth is what heals

And maybe the devil
Or evil
Or whatever you want to call it
Is lies
And lies are what hurt

And maybe that's it
Truth
And lies
That's all there is

'TWAS THE TWENTIES

'Tis the season
Of changing all the wrong things
At least that's what my twenties were for me
I changed
Where I worked
Where I lived
How I looked
Who I loved
I changed
Who I was
By any external, ironic means
I climbed mountains of undue stress
But I saw extraordinary places
I otherwise never would have seen

TWENTIES

I love the girl
I was in my twenties
She paved the way for me
Even though she couldn't see it
She was so afraid of time
Always desperately trying
To make something of herself
Before she aged out of her prime
But that wasn't her prime
Not even close
And I'm glad she didn't know
Because if she had
She wouldn't have made the mistakes
I needed to make
To learn the important things
I needed to learn
To grow

UNDERSTANDING EACH OTHER

There's total darkness
Inside of me
Inside my body
Especially inside my mind
No one else
Will ever be able to see what's inside
Without shining their own light

Anna Barba Stettler

VERDICT

I wish everyone who was desperate
Had a fair and just jury
In their head
The jury's verdict
Would be that the desperate can't end it
And they'd cite lack of evidence
They don't have enough relevant information yet

WHAT THEY THINK

He cared so much for them
That he didn't have the time
Or energy
Or room
To concern himself
With what they thought of him
And in turn
And turn again
They thought the world of him

WE THINK WE CAN'T TELL ANYONE
SO WE DON'T KNOW

We think we're crazy
We think we're fucked in the head
But so many times
The dark parts of our mind
That we think we have to hide
Make perfect sense
Like the way we play
A bit of everyone's parts in our dreams
Of course we do
We're projecting them
Directing them
Unconsciously choreographing the scenes
Or how the graphic thoughts
Of how easy it would be
To kill our new babies
Make us feel undeserving and unqualified
To even be alive
Let alone parent a child
When really
Perfectly naturally
In the only way they know how
Our minds are just coping
With the shit-ton of responsibility we have now

WEATHER

The weather is unpredictable
In my head
There's no warning
When the forecast is hazy
And when I lose sight of where I'm going
I become the storm
I go crazy

WHEN THE DANGER IS ALREADY INSIDE

You can prepare for danger
Work to become
Stronger
Faster
Smarter
Learn to decide
When to fight
When to run
When to hide
But what can you do
When the scariest place in the world
Is your mind?

WHEN THEY DECIDE TO GO

I think some of them know
When they decide to go
The world was in fact
Better for their good
I think it's their past
And especially future mistakes
That make them so afraid
And convince them that they should
They know
They'll crush the ones they love
If they choose to leave
But their clouded vision
Makes that seem
Like the lesser evil
Than the bad they *could* do
And the burden they *could* be

Anna Barba Stettler

WHEN YOU STRETCH THEIR TRUTH THEY'LL SHRINK

His mom was always proud of him
For exactly who he was
She was just insecure
She never meant to say
His truth wasn't good enough
When she exaggerated his accomplishments
But that's what he heard

WHERE SHE WENT

She never really wanted to run away
But she needed to know
There was someone who would blink
When they saw her go

WHY

Dream your big dreams
My baby
Dream as big as the sky
Just think it through
Because when your dreams come true
I know they will and when they do
The only thing that will matter to you
Is *why*

WHY THEIR GUIDE DIDN'T WORK

They could write perfect directions
Leading you down their road to success
Every curve and bump and fork accounted for
And sometimes they do
They might even try to sell it to you
But know
That their road
Won't take you where you want to go
You can learn from them
But every path to success is unique
And you have to forge your own

WIDE EYES

Born with eyes shut tight
She blinked
And her mind opened entirely
She saw nothing but an untainted blur of possibility
But she grew
Her eyes opened and her vision cleared
She learned of evil and earthly limitations
And her mind closed
Little by little
Day by day
Until she had a child of her own
Born with eyes shut tight
But when her child blinked
Her mind opened entirely
Only this time her eyes were open too
And all the magic she'd ever once believed in
Turned out to be true

WILL IT BE ALL-IMPORTANT FOREVER?

Think back
To all the different things
That felt all-important
All-consuming in the moment
You might even need to remind yourself
Of what you were so broken up about
And that might help
With whatever's eating you now

WORDS FOR ANXIETY

Some people say
The way anxiety feels
Is impossible to describe
Some people haven't
Downed a double dose of diet pills
One too many times

THE WORLD IS BRIGHT

The world is bright
Between the sun and the moon and the lights
We can see most of the time
It feels like a conspiracy
But it's not
The light isn't a distraction
From what lies beyond
It is out there, though
The infinite abyss of darkness
That we can feel inside of us
Because we're part of it
But the world
Is what matters in this life
And the world is bright

YOU DON'T UNDERSTAND

They're so fast
To say
You don't understand
They believe it too
It's funny
In the way that burns your throat
Instead of making you laugh
If only they knew
If only they knew the half

YOUR GOD GAVE UP THE POWER TO MAKE EVERYTHING OKAY

You don't have to tell yourself
That this happened to you for a reason
Even if your faith is unwaveringly strong
Others will
Of course
But they (unintentionally) lack empathy
And they're wrong
Your god
Opened you up to the traumas
Of being human
But this
It wasn't some divine design
Your god didn't do it

YOUR THINKING SPOT

When you don't feel anything
And you need it the most
There's a place for you
Out there somewhere
That will make you feel again
And I hope you can go
And if you can't
Because of anything
Or everything
Or nothing
Let it be enough
Just to know

Made in the USA
Middletown, DE
12 May 2022

65640528R00123